WYATT TEE WALKER

SPIRITS THAT DWELL IN DEEP WOODS III

The Prayer and Praise Hymns of the Black Religious Experience

Musical Notations and Arrangements

by

C. Eugene Cooper

with a foreword

by

DR. JEREMIAH A. WRIGHT, JR.

MARTIN LUTHER KING FELLOWS PRESS

SPIRITS THAT DWELL IN DEEP WOODS III

Copyright 1991

Martin Luther King Fellows Press New York, N.Y.

Library of Congress Cataloging in Publication Data

Walker, Wyatt Tee
  Spirits That Dwell in Deep Woods III
  1. Afro-American Music, 2. Afro-American Music of the Black Church, 3. Afro-American Folklore, includes notes.

LC 91-61639
ISBN 0-937644-11-0

Design: Ray Leonardo
Front cover design: Wyatt Tee Walker
Copy Editor: Judith Price
Typeset in Trump 12pt.

Printed and bound by Ray Leonardo & Sons, Valhalla, New York

The name MARTIN LUTHER KING FELLOWS PRESS is registered as a trademark in the U.S. patent office.

LK   Printed in the U.S.A.

ii

DEDICATION

To all of the
SILVER STRANDS
past and present
from whose memory banks
this treasure was mined
and especially to
Mother Eleanora Springer
who now sleeps after 101 years
of Christian Living

ACKNOWLEDGEMENTS

My debt is great. I am continually astounded by the profound theological insights contained in the literature of this music. The unnamed poets whose hearts and minds ached for justice and freedom, found solace in these faith-songs as they hoped for a better day. The legacy is rich and rife with Bible lore that nourished their hungry spirits. The simple beauty of their creations deepens our affection and respect for their indomitability of spirit.

I am mindful of a contemporary debt. The elders of this present generation who managed to survive the diasporas of the South and made their dwelling place in the urban North, sufficiently remembered the faith of their mothers and fathers to keep these hymns alive until this moment. God's name be praised for them also.

Much of the present collection of Prayer and Praise Hymns are the collective contributions of the Silver Strands who have shared a ministry of song with so many audiences in the greater New York community. It is from that sharing that at least three volumes have developed. Special thanks to the Chairman of Canaan's Official Board, Elmo Cooper, who has frequently provided this author with lyrics and melodies that have all but disappeared from current use. Deacon Cooper, a native of Florida, possesses a special gift of memory and faith that has enhanced this effort at many points.

I am especially grateful to the Reverend Paul Lowe of Richmond, Virginia who made available to me some very old hymns of this family of music which have helped me immeasurably in completing this third volume. I am grateful to my collaborator, C. Eugene Cooper, who has provided the musical notations for these hymns in four-part harmony, carefully preserving them as near as possible in their pristine form. Judith Price, once again, has served as copy editor and manuscript typist, Diane Price, has been patient in the several typings necessary to prepare the final typescript for publication. Theresa Ann Walker, my wife and sweetheart of forty-one years, has been good enough to read the early manuscript and offered suggestions which made this a better work than it might have been.

The congregation of the Canaan Baptist Church of Christ has provided me with an environment that encourages me to do worthwhile tasks that stretch my mind and spirit. I am thankful for the continuing inspiration they afford me as I serve them as Pastor and friend.

Wyatt Tee Walker
Harlem, New York
April, 1991

AUTHOR'S PREFACE
to Volume III

The initial idea for this work began with only a title in 1979. The foreword to my seminal work in this field, *Somebody's Calling My Name*, was written by that prince of preachers, Gardner C. Taylor of Brooklyn's Concord Church. In the body of his comments, Dr. Taylor included a quote from Booker T. Washington's autobiography, *Up From Slavery*. It was part of a narrative describing his early childhood in the slave quarters. Seated around fires at night, they contemplated their lot and sang of many things - "war, hunting and *spirits that dwell in deep woods.*"

That haunting phrase arrested my attention in gripping fashion. At the time, I was unable to decipher the mystique of its spell over me. However, I resolved that I would use that quote as a title for some future work about the music of the Black religious experience. My continuing research and interest in the music of our religious tradition soon led me to consider the *Prayer and Praise Hymns* of the North American religious experience. I determined that this phrase would be an apt if not perfect title for what I proposed to do. In May of 1985, the first volume of a three volume work was published.

There is something mystical and ethereal about this quote from the pen of Booker T. Washington which hands cannot grasp and tongue cannot taste. It is of the Spirit.

In my earlier work, I had carefully (I thought) traced the development of Black Sacred Music. In the course of completing a doctoral dissertation, it occurred to me that *this* body of music was distinct from all others that I had included in my typology. They were deserving of their own niche and identity! I fastened upon them the label, *Prayer and Praise Hymns* because of their function in the religious practice of Christians of African descent. Thus, the *Spirits* series was born.

The schema remains the same both in terms of the selection of the hymn *types* and the individual exposition of each hymn. Once again, I have treated a modest variety of theological ideas, hymn tunes and geographical representation. The breadth is more flexible than wooden. The exposition of the individual hymn begins with a brief introductory word followed by comment on its *Biblical Basis, Theological Mooring, Lyric* and *Form Analysis* and *Contemporary Significance.*

With intentionality, I remain a collector and would appreciate any sharing of words and/or music of hymns of this genre by those who read this pioneer effort to place in permanent form another expression of the oral tradition that remains extant in North America.*

Wyatt Tee Walker
Harlem, New York
April 1991

*Identical to Preface of Volume II

FOREWORD

The haunting, powerful, mysterious and hypnotic strands of music from the Black Sacred Music tradition have long been recognized as one of God's most visible (or *audible*) signs of His abiding presence and unfailing promise in the midst of the pain predicament of Africans living in the North American diaspora. God who promised never to leave nor forsake us is present in the African-American predicament; and His presence is felt poignantly in the *Prayer and Praise Hymns* of these people.

God was known by Africans long before the first Muslim slave ship carried them across the Indian Ocean in the East African slave trade and long before the first Christian slave ship carried them across the Atlantic Ocean in the West African slave trade; and this same God who "sits high and looks low" is a God of justice, love and mercy. He is also is a God who is "writing all the time", and there is nothing that escapes His attention. It is *this* God of whom the Africans living in diaspora sing in their Prayer and Praise tradition; and it is of this God and these songs that Dr. Wyatt Tee Walker writes.

Following his first work, *Somebody's Calling My Name* in which he chronicled the Black Sacred Music tradition from the days of the spiritual throught the songs of the Civil Rights Movement, Walker's next two volumes on music picked up a lesser known *genre* and began an exposure and an anlysis that has been most beneficial to students of the Africans American religious tradition, to ethnomusicologists and to scholars in the theological tradition of Africans who live in the diaspora. The Prayer and Praise Hymn *genre* is not a well known *genre* to most African Americans who live in Northern metropolitan areas. As Walker's introductions to each song indicate, most (if not all) of these songs are songs from the South where the prayer and praise tradition produced a music that is unknown to most Northerners under the age of 50.

ix

With that period in African American church history that Gayraud Wilmore calls "the deradicalization of the black church", and that Joseph Washington classifies the "bourgeousification" of the black church, there came in Northern church circles the desparate, futile, foolish and inane attempt to "whitenize" our worship services. Along with the Eurocentric focus came the elimination of Southern, "country" practices like Prayer and Praise Hymns, common meter hymns (or "Dr. Watts" songs) and shape note singing. As a result, many younger African Americans who grew up in the North have never heard these songs that Walker lifts from Southern and rural obscurity. Almost no younger Northerner has heard them in their original *Sitz im Leben* unless they have relatives "down home" and have gone South for family reunions, homecomings, camp meetings (revivals) or holidays.

We owe Dr. Walker a great debt of gratitude for his extensive work in this field, for his insightful analysis and for his painstaking research. The theological interpretations he gives (as well as the contemporary implications) help the untutored reader to begin to appreciate the breadth and depth of African American thought, and the profundity of the "common folk" as they grappled with Biblical issues and the paradoxical complexities of being black (oppressed) *and* Christian.

God as seen by those who are on the underside of society is *not* the same God as seen by those who are "on top". The religion of the slave and the religion of the slave holder are by definition two different religions; and the gods that they serve are by extension two different gods. The God of Africans in diaspora is consistent with the God of the Bible who enters into history on the side of the oppressed, in the corner of those "on the underside", and fighting the cause of the slaves and the descendants of slaves.

It is this God that is prayed to and praised in these songs Walker analysis. It is this God who is sung to and sung about in brush arbors, hush arbors, and wooden frame country churches. It is this God who is felt moving in the mysterious music of a people whose spirits cannot be crushed; and it is to this God that we say:

> To God Be The Glory
> For The Things God Has Done

The Rev. Dr. Jeremiah A. Wright, Jr.
Trinity United Church of Christ
Chicago, Illinois
May, 1991

TABLE OF CONTENTS

INTRODUCTION

The *Prayer and Praise Hymns* have been an integral part of the sacred hymnody of the Afro-American religious experience. Following the disappointment of the Post-reconstruction era, African-American religious practice turned increasingly inward. Though the children of slaves borrowed from and adapted some of the worship styles of the dominant society(whites), the practical reality of the separateness in American life induced in Christians of African ancestry, a form of self-reliance so far as the character of our worship styles were concerned. Black people trudged ahead with their Africanized version of Christianity, coping as best we could with the persistent presence of racism and color prejudice.

Emigration from the rural South was not widespread. At the turn of the century large numbers of African Americans remained in the countryside working the land they owned or sharecropping. It was in the rural South, principally, that these hymns were born.

These hymns are not *Spirituals* in either the technical or historical sense. All authentic *Spirituals* antedated the end of the Civil War. Neither are they *Black Meter Music* in any sense, though much of the verbiage is drawn from the bright imagery of the latter part of the meter music era. They are adaptations of what rural Afro-Americans heard around them religiously. The poetry and musicality of the *Prayer and Praise Hymns* are distinct from that of *Spirituals* and *Black Meter Music*.

In time frame, these songs are spin-offs of the early hymn book era in Black religious life (c. 1885-1925). They are in every sense, folk-music of the Black religious experience. Like the *Spirituals* in this respect, there are no identifiable authors. The body of this music expresses in individual form the collective consciousness of the community in matters of religious belief. There is in this music the flavor of both the *Spiritual* and *Black Meter Music* without any real loss of its own identity.

The primary purpose of this introductory word is to provide a general profile of this music-form to avoid unnecessary repetition in the body of the general text. The several parts of this profile are applicable to nearly all of the hymns of this music family

There are no hymns which are not *Bible-Based*. It is not difficult to fix the explicit and/or implicit references in the Scriptures. This is no surprise given the influence of the *Spirituals* in the musicality of the African-American community generally and in religious life particularly. The practice of religion among Americans of African descent on the North American continent reveals clearly that we are essentially people of the Book. Our religious faith and practice centers in the authority of the Bible.

All of these songs are of *southern origin*. At the beginning of the twentieth century, no mass migrations to the industrial centers of the North had yet taken place. The predominant population of African Americans remained in the South and border states. There had been as noted earlier, measurable shifts of population to the urban centers of the South but not in sufficient numbers to deplete the rural areas of a sizable Black community.

The character of this music betrays its rural roots. The repetition, which we shall turn to in a moment, reveals that the *oral tradition* was still operative. Its presence was as much out of need as it was cultural for Afro-Americans in the rural South. In spite of freedom schools and literacy training, many, many New World Africans were barely literate. The hymnbook was coming into broad use after the turn of the century, but literacy rates were abysmally low in the rural. These hymns of faith are by no means the product of an urban environment. Their formation was distinct and separate from piano and organ accompaniment.

The *repetitive character* to which we have already alluded, served primarily as a memory device for these rural residents of the South who had very narrow access to literacy training. Again, the meager resources in the rural South made the likelihood of hymnbooks rare and the purchase of pianos and organs even more rare. This repetitive quality is a direct descendant of the *Spiritual's* influence whose antecedent was the repetitive music of West Africa. All are tied together in the tradition of oral transmission with repetition being one of its primary devices.

The *restricted literary* form was directly influenced by the repetitive character. Rhyme was only of secondary importance. The most frequently occurring poetic forms are the *a a a b* and the *a a b a*. Next in frequency is the *ab ab ab ab* and the double *a a a b*. Occasionally, there is also *a a b c a* and *a b a c* with variations of the others noted above.

Nearly half of these praise hymns extant make broad use of

the traveling couplet and the quatrain form for stanza material. The traveling couplet form was born with the *Spirituals* and used in precisely the same random manner. The quatrain form was introduced to frontier America by the fabled Dr. Isaac Watts and the Wesley brothers, John and Charles. African Americans "borrowed" what was useful and attractive to their spiritual appetites.

The musical modality of these hymns is similar. Most of the melodies can be charted on the *pentatonic scale* (five notes). With rare exception, the music is *rhythmic* though there are a few numbers that are measured and slow moving. The imagery is in the folk-idiom drawn from the everyday experiences of the plain and simple people of the land who gave birth to this family of music. All are *testimonial* in character and deeply personalized as evidence of God's encounter with their lives.

In the body of this work, each hymn selected is analyzed individually. Each has its own message mnd witness in song. The chapters begin with the musical notation in four part harmony facing the full lyrics (so far as possible) on the page opposite. The narrative accompanying the hymn opens with a brief word of introduction to that specific hymn. There follows the general exposition that includes the *Biblical Basis*, the *Theological Mooring*, *Lyric and Form Analysis* and *Contemporary Significance.* *

---

*Author's Note: This *Introduction* is essentially the same introduction to Volume I of *Spirits That Dwell In Deep Woods* with only minor editorial changes.

BORN AGAIN

SOMETHING HAPPENED WHEN HE SAVED ME

Notations are charted as sung by Silver Strands

2

SOMETHING HAPPENED WHEN HE SAVED ME

Refrain

Something happened when He Saved me,
It happened in my heart,
It made my soul rejoice;
Something happened when He saved me,
Something happened in my heart.

It was Monday when He saved me,
It happened in my heart,
It made my soul rejoice;
Something happened when He saved me,
Something happened in my heart.

It was Tuesday when He saved me,
It happened in my heart,
It made my soul rejoice;
Something happened when He saved me,
Something happened in my heart.

It was Wednesday when He saved me,
It happened etc.

It was Thursday etc.

It was Friday etc.

It was Saturday etc.

It was Sunday etc.

3

BORN AGAIN

Something Happened When He Saved Me

Introduction

During the Freedom Ride in 1961, I was unceremoniously jailed by Sheriff Mack Charles Butler in Montgomery, Alabama. Ralph and Juanita Abernathy's home had become the headquarters for the "resumed" Freedom Ride. It had been interrupted by the vicious violence of the racists in collusion with the police establishment under Butler's command. Bernard Lee, Abernathy and I had escorted some professors and students from New England universities to the Greyhound bus terminal for their next leg of the journey to Jackson, Mississippi. It was in this circumstance that the arrest occurred. We routinely refused bail and remained in jail for three days until Dr. King determined that our being in jail was unproductive at this stage of the Freedom Ride. It was during this brief stay that I was first introduced to this hymn.

Abernathy was a native of Marengo County, Alabama and since I heard it first from him, I have assumed it has Alabama roots. In recent years, I have found residents of both Birmingham and Montgomery who were thoroughly familier with this rare-form hymn.

Even though the poetic form is different from most hymns of this genre, it does fit the round-style class of this family *of music*. The *round-style* hymn (cg. *Spirits I & II*) is so named because all are characterized by the *Monday, Tuesday, Wednesday, etc.* phenomenon. It is indeed a special kind of *Prayer and Praise Hymn*.

Biblical Basis

The singular unique teaching of the field preacher from Galilee centers in the *new birth*. Jesus' late night meeting with Nicodemus the Pharisee, placed the concept of being *born again* as the linch-pin experience of every Christian.[1] The Apostle Paul in his Corinthian correspondence provided continuity to the idea of the second birth with his clear statement, *"Therefore, if any man be in Christ, he is a new creature: old things are passed away; behold all things are become new."*[2] So central is this unique teaching of the *second birth* that in our own era, the verbal test of Christian conversion is the declaration of the *second birth*. Over the last thirty years, the majority community in America has been awash with a new sense of being *born again* Christians. It must be said that in the African-American free church tradition, being *born again* has always been the prerequisite for entrance into the fellowship of any church.

It is then understandable, that in a collection of *Prayer and Praise Hymns*, there will predictably be a number of hymns that give expression to the conversion experience. In every family of music, whether *Spiritual, Prayer and Praise Hymn or Gospel* testimony concerning being *born again* find expression again and again.[3] The centrality of Jesus in African-American religious experience precludes that the idea of the *second birth* would have some considerable prominence in its music irrespective of the era of which it issues.

Theological Mooring

The words of Jesus as reported in the Gospel of John constitute the theological basis for this *Prayer and Praise Hymn*.[4] As indicated in the previous section, the Apostle Paul, in closer proximity to the apostolic tradition than the

Gospel record itself, complements the concept in II Corinthians 5:17. There is absolutely no quarrel that the *second birth* was an integral part of the New Testiment church tradition and became firmly established as a part of the entrance requirement into *the Way,* as the early Church described itself. Both the writings of Paul and the Gospel tradition link the *born again* experience with the rite of baptism by immersion. Thereby, the New Testiment Church tradition unto the present time mark the *new birth* by water baptism. Of course, in the high Church, the practice is not as pronounced.

It is patently clear whomever comes to Christ as a disciple must *"confess with thy mouth the Lord Jesus Christ, and shalt believe in thy heart that God raised him from the dead* in order to lay hands upon eternal life.[5] Though Paul does not use the precise verbiage of John's gospel, the meaning of being a *new creature in Christ* is without any difference whatsoever. At the heart of Jesus' conversation with Nicodemus and Paul's treatise to the Roman church is the reality that accepting Jesus as Lord involves taking on a new morality that is often contrary to the norm of the world. This *Prayer and Praise Hymn* testifies to that long-standing tradition that conversion in Jesus Christ changes one's life forever.

Lyric and Form Analysis

Compared with other *Prayer and Praise Hymns,* this music-piece is distinct both in its poetic form and melodic frame. It violates slightly the stated profile of slavish loyalty to the pentatonic scale.[6] However, there are enough remaining characteristics for it to be classified as an authentic part of the genre of music of African-American religious expression. Admittedly, the time parameters of the creation of this music provide ample opportunity for increased sophistication and *borrowing* which might have easily contributed to this hymn's distinctness.[7] The musicality does not quite possess the flavor of most of the music under

7

scrutiny. However, this hymn requires our attention under this grouping for reasons that are obvious in its overall construct.

> a *Something happened when He saved me,*
> b *It happened in my heart,*
> c *It made my soul rejoice;*
> a *Something happened when He saved me,*
> d *Something happened in my heart.*

The charting above displays a poetic form that appears to be so different from all others previously reviewed that it seems foreign. At this writing, despite charting more than one hundred and fifty of these hymns, this author has no explanation for this sharp variation in form other than to note the difference and accept it as it is. I am not so sure that any explanation is needed or required.

So far as the musical piece itself is concerned, the chief difference has been noted. It is that melodic departure which might prohibit this hymn from being so quickly adaptable to communal use as some others. The melodic line is noticeably a little more intricate in construction than the other hymns considered so far. Both its form and musical structure provide adequate ground for interest and conjecture.

Contemporary Significance

The conversion experience in the African-American religious experience has always been central in the life of confessing Christians. It is similar to other life experiences that have deep subjective meaning in that, the more distant in time the event, the more embellished the details become. That fact notwithstanding, the conversion event usually remains uppermost in the consciousness of Christians of African ancestry. Most can recite the day, the place and the hour and some of the circumstances that surrounded the event. In times of great stress and spiritual trauma, it is the conversion experience that is called upon to shore up broken hearts and repentant spirits. It is the universal reference point of the faith journey. It follows then, that this hymn-poem possesses great value because it internalizes for the individual *and* the group, a moment in the worshipper's religious life with which everyone else in the faith-family can identify. Its value is enhanced by this particular form which provides an opportunity for everyone present to relive that moment by standing on his or her *day*. That memory in that instant has been known to re-charge spiritual batteries that were low and inspire marginal Christians to meaningful discipleship. The message of this hymn is clear and powerful: Personal salvation in Jesus Christ has been a change of the heart that has induced joy in the soul.

> *"When I think about the goodness of Jesus,*
> *And all that He's done for me;*
> *My soul cries out, Hallelujah!*
> *Thank God for saving me!"*[8]

Notes

1. John 3:1ff
2. II Corinthians 5:17
3. John 3:3
4. Ibid
5. Romans 10:9
6. see *Introduction*, p. 3
7. c. 1885-1925
8. Traditional hymn

SO GLAD RELIGION

ANOTHER DAY'S JOURNEY AND I'M SO GLAD

Notations are charted as sung by Silver Strands

ANOTHER DAY'S JOURNEY AND I'M SO GLAD

Refrain

Another day's journey and I'm so glad!
Another day's journey and I'm so glad!
Another day's journey and I'm so glad!
And the world can't do me no harm.

Beat the devil running and I'm so glad!
Beat the devil running and I'm so glad!
Beat the devil running and I'm so glad!
And the world can't do me no harm.

Got good religion and I'm so glad!
Got good religion and I'm so glad!
Got good religion and I'm so glad!
And the world can't do me no harm.

Feel the fire burning and I'm so glad!
Feel the fire burning and I'm so glad!
Feel the fire burning and I'm so glad!
And the world can't do me no harm.

I'm on my way to heaven and I'm so glad!
I'm on my way to heaven and I'm so glad!
I'm on my way to heaven and I'm so glad!
And the world can't do me no harm.

l

22

SO GLAD RELIGION

Another Day's Journey And I'm So Glad

Introduction

Though the melodic and poetic ground of this family of music is narrow, the breadth of ideas expressed, is of considerable variety. This *Prayer and Praise Hymn* sounds a clear theme on the providence of God both in immediate and eschatological terms. It is as immediate as today's *journey* and as eschatological as the ultimate goal of the follower of Christ -*heaven*- eternal life. The spirited refrain of this *Prayer and Praise Hymn* is without regional boundaries. It is familier to any and all assemblies of worshipping Christians of African descent in the free Church tradition. Its primary venue of use has been in revival settings and evangelistic meetings. The lyrics of the closing line in the repeating refrain are reminiscent of the discussion in Chapter 5 concerning the bliblical tradition of the view of a personal devil. Most pronounced is the *testimonial* character of the music-piece itself in terms of the awareness of God's presence and the accompanying joy that personal trust in God insulates the devotee from all *hurt, harm and danger* that the forces of evil may try impose.

Biblical Basis

The seed thought of this *Prayer and Praise Hymn* can be

traced directly to the Sermon on the Mount. These sayings of Jesus embrace a startling code of ethics when compared to what is the norm in contemporary society. Against the backdrop of Judaism, it derided the cold legalism of the scribes and the Pharisees. The specific teaching on which this hymn rests is our Lord's admonition to take *one day at a time*:

> *Take no thought for your life what ye eat*
> *or what ye shall drink; nor yet for the body*
> *what ye shall put on. Is not life more than*
> *meat and the body more than raiment...*
> *Take therefore no thought for the morrow; for*
> *the morrow shall take thought for the things*
> *of itself.*[1]

The words of Jesus challenge our trust in Him. In this same passage, the Crucified Carpenter reminds us that God takes care of birds and surely we are more precious than *the fowls of the air.*[2]

It is likely that our ancestors in the meagerness of their existence, developed a keener sense of trust and dependence on God than we can appropriate for ourselves in our indulgent bent toward materialism. It is interesting to note that the hymn's testimony is devoid of any mention of that which smacks of *getting and spending.* It speaks concretely of that which is lasting, the spiritual values that sustain life; God's providence, resistance to temptation, meaningful faith, the zeal of commitment and the fixed destination of eternal life. *Another Day's Journey* expresses a valuable guide for Christian discipleship.

Theological Mooring

The fundamental theological tenet underscored by this music-piece is the believer's necessary dependence on God's providence. We cannot know the future and we can only live one day at a time. Its lyrics are explicit in reciting the tests of daily living as a Christian. The structure of the hymn is balanced by the recurring phrase, *I'm so glad* but theologically posits the attitude of the true believer — joy and fulfillment in the service of the Lord. Too many Christians have allowed their commitment of faith to become drudgery. The Lucan narrative of the Prodigal Son reveals the sin of the elder brother who remained at home but failed his father by becoming a drudge.[3] There was no joy in his sonship!

Unless there is a high level of contentment in our servantship to Jesus Christ, our discipleship will wax and wane. It is the glue of faith. Life's pathway is often uneven and precarious and without a sense of fulfillment, we become easy prey to temptation and worse, falling away from the fellowship that is in Jesus Christ.

In specific terms of the theology expressed, the central ideas found in the closing line of each stanza and the phrase at the end of the changing stanza line. The *world can't do me no harm* closing line induces emphasis by sheer repetition. The theological sense is that the true believer who depends on God's providence, resists the temptation of the world, remains faithful to his or her religious commitment and whose zeal is like *fire*, will be fully insulated from the powers of evil. It is another reminder of Paul's message in Romans that the faithful are *free from the power of sin!*[4]

The repeating phrase, *I'm so glad* in each stanza bespeaks a fundamental posture of the devotee in his or her faith — the joy of discipleship. That attitude has already been examined at the beginning of this section.

Lyric and Form Analysis

It has been mentioned in an earlier work (*Spirits II*) that this music developed without any hard and fast rules of composition. The folk-character of this genre of Afrocentric religious expression presumes great freedom of form. Even though there are some constants in the profile of this music (see *Introduction*) exceptions abound. At several points, this writer has set forth that in most instances, *the refrain establishes the character* of the hymn-poem.[5] Here we have an exception. In truth, there is no refrain *per se* of this hymn. The form of this hymn has no internal or external suggestion that there is any need to return to the beginning stanza. In this wise, it is similar in construction to *Daniel in the Lions' Den.*[6]

Despite the exception in form noted above, in poetic form, theis *Prayer and Praise hymn* reverts to type. It is the classic *a a a b* form so common to this familo of music.

> *a   Another day's journey and I'm so glad!*
> *a   Another day's journey and I'm so glad!*
> *a   Another day's journey and I'm so glad!*
> *b   And the world can't do me no harm.*

Perhaps it is instructive to note that unlike many other hymns of this genre, the poetic form does not change from stanza to stanza. Usually, at least one line in the poetic form is sacrificed in order to accommodate the stanza construction (cf. *I Wanna' Die Easy* or *Till I Die*).

The testimonial character of this hymn is obvious though like many others, its personal cast (*And the world can't do me no harm.*) does not preclude the collective sense of the community. It is with considerable frequency that the reader will find an individual expression that speaks for the group.

Contemporary Significance

The pell-mell pace of modern living is fraught with many dangers. Most of the dangers are more spiritual than physical. It is true that there is, at this moment, appropriate concern about reducing the stress in our lives and the medical profession has detailed the harmful effects of stressful living on our mental and physical health. However, these ill effects are only of temporal concern. The spiritual dangers reach beyond the grave. It behooves the followers of the Lord Jesus Christ to be prudent in guarding against these spiritual dangers as well as those which are physical and mental.

Anxiety is at the heart of the danger. An exaggerated

concern about the future, *getting and spending*, can quickly induce in confessing Christians the wrong focus in our lives. The cliche is somewhat hackneyed but true: the Christian must focus on making a life, not a living. It is the arena of *getting and spending* that we are most prone to be tempted away from that which Jesus Christ demands of us. The danger is that we shall be overtaken by *wants* instead of merely satisfying *needs*.

As we make our way through this life, we must be convinced that our lives were never meant to wander up and down the back-alleys of life, *getting and spending*, but God created us for a specific, higher purpose. That purpose is to find life's meaning and destiny through Him who is our Saviour. *Another Day's Journey* provides clear focus for that task.

Notes

1. Matthew 6:28
2. Luke 12:24
3. Luke 15:25-32
4. Roman 6ff
5. see Chapter Three, *Till I Die*
6. Wyatt Tee Walker, *Spirits That Dwell in Deep Woods II* (New York: Martin Luther King Fellows Press, 1987), p. 75

HOLDING ON

TILL I DIE, TILL I DIE

Notations are charted as sung by Silver Strands

Aztec® PT – 8 R

DIAZ-TEC 500

TILL I DIE, TILL I DIE

Refrain

Till I die, till I die,
Till I die, till I die,
I'm gonna' keep on serving ma' Jesus,
Till I die.

Got my han' on the Gospel plow,
Wouldn't give nothin' for ma' journey now.
I'm gonna' keep on serving ma' Jesus
Till I die.

Struggling hard to make it in,
Duckin' Satan and dodgin' sin.
I'm gonna' keep on serving ma' Jesus
Till I die.

My whole life is in the freedom fight,
Can't stop now 'cause I know it's right.
I'm gonna keep on serving ma' Jesus
Till I die.

Goin' up to heav'n to see my Lord,
I can't miss for it's in His word.
I'm gonna' keep on serving ma' Jesus
Till I die.

HOLDING ON

Till I Die, Till I Die

Introduction

The primary ingredient in Christian discipleship is faithfulness. Those who romanticize and sentimentalize the Christian way have not clearly perceived kingdom service. The words of the Nazerene himself, repeatedly made clear the arduous and onerous character of discipleship.[1] True discipleship cannot be prosecuted without unbridled faithfulness. There is no way to know the future, consequently, whoever labors in the service of the King of kings must be prepared to face any obstacle, endure any trial and absorb any pain in following the Lord Christ. The religion of Jesus of Nazareth is not suited to wimps.

This *Prayer and Praise Hymn* echoes the admonition of Revelation. Faithfulness *unto death* is the prerequisite to receive *a crown of life.*[2] Both the refrain and the stanzas make clear the perseverance — the ultimate resolve of faith — is the key to kingdom entry. A religious folk-saying of an earlier day reveals that all else is vain unless one *holds out and proves faithful to the end.*

Biblical Basis

The virtue of perseverance has a decidely New Testament emphasis. During the early Galilean campaign, Jesus' response to an excuse from unequivocal discipleship appears harsh: *"No man having put his hand to the plough, and looking back, is fit for the kingdom."*³ Perseverance in the kingdom teaching of Jesus particularly and the New Testament generally, is thematic. Consequently, a random choice could be made as the biblical basis for the ground of this hymn.

Paul's second letter to the church at Corinth has a passage that suitably matches the theme of this *Prayer and Praise Hymn:*

> *We are troubled on every side, yet not*
> *distressed; we are perplexed, but not*
> *in despair;*
> *Persecuted, but not forsaken, cast down*
> *but now destroyed;*⁴

The essence of Paul's declaration and the message of this hymn are the same. *No matter what happens, our perseverance in the service of Jesus Christ is unto death!* The repeating line is a transparent clue to its central message: *I'm gonna' keep on servng ma' Jesus, Till I die.*

The stanzas, individually, bespeak Bible origin. The first stanza is an explicit reference to the teaching of Jesus already mentioned. The second stanza personalizes evil in the figure of Satan as he is portrayed in both the Old and New Testament. Satan's conversation with God in the Job narrative and the Temptation of Christ are two examples that come immediately to mind. The third stanza might well be an interpolation of recent days though it is not too far-fetched to presume that it could be a part of the original composition since the antebellum and postwar community viewed Jesus as *Liberator.*⁵ The fourth stanza's reference, *I can't miss for it's in His Word* may be a direct reference to Revelation 2:10: *. . .be thou faithful unto death, and I will give thee a crown of life.* All in all, this *Prayer and Praise Hymn* lifts up clearly the New Testament teaching that entrance into the kingdom of heaven turns on perseverance of the faithful.

Theological Mooring

It is a given that all religious disciplines require some level of faith from their devotees. The religion of Jesus Christ is distinct from all others because of the ethics and morality that are tied directly to belief. The Apostle Paul's treatise on salvation to the church at Rome is explicit on this question. *He who through faith is righteous is saved!*[6] In lay terms, the believer's acceptance of the grace of God which is in Jesus Christ requires a specific response in behavior. In simple terms, following Jesus Christ presumes participation in a *salvation ethic.* Thus genuine faith translates into conduct. That conduct is grounded in unconditional and non-conditional faith. The Book of Hebrews declares, . . .*without faith it is impossible to please Him: for he that cometh to God must believe He is, and that He is a rewarder of them that diligently seek Him.*[7]

This hymn is rooted in the tradition of that faith described above. It is the faith of Abraham as well as the faith of John on Patmos. The poetic frame of the hymn is clear-sighted; *perseverance* is the key to kingdom entry irrespective of the reality of temptation and struggle. That *perseverance* concept is buried in the repeating line and re-emphasized in the plow metaphor. The verbiage, *struggling hard* and *duckin Satan and dodgin' sin* mirror our human frailty. The inclusion of the *freedom fight* raises a dimension of Christian faith often ignored and obscured, the demand for justice. The last stanza includes the obligatory eschatological piece necessary to any authentic Christian expression of faith.

Lyric and Form Analysis

Till I Die is the epitome of the most frequent poetic form common to the *Prayer and Praise* hymns. It is cast in the *a a b a* frame. The author exercises some mild perogative in determining that the last line is essentially the same as the two beginning lines though the repetition of the phrase, *Till I die* is absent. I think the reader will agree that this decision, so far as form analysis, represents no significant change. The option would be to consider the last line a distinct line unto itself which seems tortuous and awkward. The poetic frame would then become *a a b c* which appears to violate the structure of the hymn itself since the words are exactly the same. The first option seems logical and appropriate.

a	*Till I die, till I die,*
a	*Till I die, till I die,*
b	*I'm gonna' keep on serving ma' Jesus*
a	*Till I die*

The stanza form is consistent though distinct from the refrain. It is a common arrangement when use of the *traveling couplet* device is utilized for verse material. There is frequent variation in the supply of stanza material then in the basic structure of the refrain itself. Usually it is the refrain which establishes the character of the hymn.

a	*Got my han' on the Gospel plow*
b	*Wouldn't take nothin' for ma' journey now*
c	*I'm gonna' keep on serving ma' Jesus*
d	*Till I die.*

The *Introduction* to this volume makes a passing comment on the *traveling couplet*.[8] This couplet device is comprised of two rhyming verses and is so named because they *travel* from song to song. This device was born with the *Spiritual's* creation and continued its life with this family of Black Sacred Music under review. Some couplets are found both in the *Spirituals* and the *Prayer and Praise Hymns*. It needs to be mentioned that the use of the couplet device in no way impairs the integrity of the hymn with which it finds use. The fair presumption is that the couplet employed amplifies the basic message of the hymn where it finds a home whether permanent or transient.

The musicality of this hymn is distinct. Many, many hymns of this family of music are similar bordering on being identical. Hymns like *Till I Die* which possess their own distinct melodic structure seem to be more enduring in their use and thus remain more stable in their original form. The others, which are similar, often suffer modifications that obscure their precise origins.

Contemporary Significance

Not enough Christians take their commitment to discipleship seriously. This *Prayer and Praise Hymn* sends a clear message to confessing Christians. The pilgrimage through this *waste-howling wilderness* of our existence requires some spiritual grit. Too many followers of the Lord Jesus Christ become faint-hearted in the face of trial and travail. It is a reproach to God and an embarassment to the faith when we whimper and fall away in time of trouble. This hymn strengthens the resolve and builds the morale of the worshipper. Christians of African descent in this moment, face troublous times. Our sociology is a disaster. Our nation plunged into a war last year in which we had no stake at all (the Gulf War). The outcome holds promise of compounding the disastrous sociology in which we remain entrapped. The financial drain induced by the war diminishes the domestic programs that affect our community most. The profile of the troops at risk were inordinately our young men and women of the minority community, too many of African ancestry! It is to this continuing reality of oppression and injustice that this hymn speaks with clarity. No matter how much our hopes and aspirations are diminished, we must develop the capacity *to serve ma' Jesus till I die!*

Notes

1. Luke 14:26-33
2. Revelation 2:10
3. II Corinthians 4:8
4. Luke 9:62
5. John Lovell, Jr., *Black Song: The Forge and the Flame* (New York: Macmillan, Inc., 1972), Chapter 17
6. Romans 1:17
7. Hebrews 11:6
8. see *Introduction*, p.3

'TIS SO SWEET

NOBODY BUT YOU LORD

No-body but you, Lord ____ No--bo-dy but you ____ No-body but

You, Lord ____ no-body but you! ____ you brought me

ov - er ____ and you brought me through ____ no-bo-dy but

You ____ Lord, No-bo-dy but you ____ No-bo-dy but

Notations are charted as sung by Silver Strands

NOBODY BUT YOU LORD

Refrain

*Nobody but you, Lord
Nobody but you!
Nobody but you, Lord
Nobody but you!
You brought me over,
(And) You brought me through!
Nobody but you, Lord,
Nobody but you!*

*When I was a sinner,
Nobody but you!
When I was a sinner,
Nobody but you!
You brought me over,
(And) You brought me through!
Nobody but you, Lord,
Nobody but you!*

*When I was in trouble,
Nobody but you!
When I was in trouble,
Nobody but you!
You brought me over,
(And) You brought me through!
Nobody but you, Lord,
Nobody but you!*

'TIS SO SWEET

Nobody But You, Lord

Introduction

This hymn first came to this writer's attention during a revival meeting at the Mt. Olive Baptist Church in Ft. Lauderdale, Florida. In conversation with the pastor, Dr. Mack King Carter, a celebrated theologian, he shared with me his mild amazement as to how much of the oral tradition persists in African-American church life. It is most dominant in the music of the free Church tradition. Mt. Olive, with all the appurtenances of contemporary church management, computers, professional staff, modern facilities, etc., yet maintains a strong, cultivated folk-church tradition. Within the fabric of worship practice, there was frequent punctuation with the genre of music under consideration.

Most congregations of the free Church tradition provide a period before the formal services for prayer, song and testimony. It was in this setting that this hymn was gleaned. It is somewhat a typical in its poetic form but very traditional in its musicality.

Biblical Basis

This simple, straightforward hymn is a classic statement of *trust*. In ancillary fashion, it is suggestive of the prevailing providence of God for those who put their trust in Him. The lyrics explicitly fix the believer's complete dependence on the goodness and mercy of God.

For all of the above, it is not dificult to fix a Biblical basis for the sentiment expressed in this testimonial hymn. The Scriptures, of course are replete with references to trust in God. The passage following from Psalm 40 embraces the thought intended.

"I waited patiently for the Lord and he
inclined his ear unto me and heard my cry.
He brought me up also out of an horrible
pit, out of the miry clay, and set my feet
upon a rock, and established my goings.
And he hath put a new song in my mouth
even praise unto our God; many shall see
it and shall trust in the Lord."[1]

The influence of narrow literacy during the era of this music's development is obvious in this hymn. The absence of explicit reference to a particular scripture does not in any way diminish its Bible root. Despite rampant illiteracy in the rural South where these hymns were coined, Christians of African descent found out what was in the Bible. Somewhere between illiteracy and rote memory of the Scriptures, the discerning religiosity of the plain and simple people of the land culled the spiritual tenets by which they survived racism and despair. As folksy as this end-product may be, it incorporates in striking manner a fundamental truth of the Christian faith.

Theological Mooring

The abiding value of the *Prayer and Praise Hymns* is the consistency with which they reveal the theological insights that are both biblically sound and theologically clear. Sometimes in the West, our approach to theology is confusing, sometimes disconcerting. This author's anlysis is that often there is insufficient clarity on what theology is as it relates to Biblical authority. The Bible is the Christian's record of God's dealing with humankind; theology is our attempt to decipher that record.

Afro-centric Christian theology proceeds from a different center than does Euro-centric theology. The theology of African-Americans issues from our pain-predicament (which has been pervasive) and thereby, more experential than reflective. Ours is a *learned* and *lived* theology. This is not to suggest that the religious faith of African-Americans is impervious to Continental theological musings but only that Afro-centricity is dominant.[2]

This hymn-poem lifts up squarely the complete dependence on God. The implicit truth is that God has responded to those who put their trust in Him through his grace (conversion) and providence (deliverance). If God cannot forgive, what hope is there for humankind's salvation? If God cannot provide deliverance, his Sovereignty is suspect. This hymn testifies that God indeed, does forive (*When I was a sinner...*) and He provides deliverance (*You brought me over (and) You brought me through...*).

God's Sovereignty and his power to deliver (Omnipotence) are theological tenets of faith certified in the biblical record. *In the beginning God created the heavens and the earth* and through Moses He delivered the children of Israel from bondage in Egypt.

Lyric and Form Analysis

The poetic structure of *Nobody but you, Lord*, is greatly similar to *Blessed Be The Name of the Lord*.[3] The Job story in song is *a b a b a b c d e*. This hymn is an *a b a b c d a b*. The similarity is apparent though *Nobody But You, Lord* has no *d* line and places the third *a b* couplet at the end of the piece.

a	*Nobody but you, Lord*
b	*Nobody but you.*
a	*Nobody but you, Lord,*
b	*Nobody but you.*
c	*You brought me over,*
d	*(And) You brought me through;*

a   *Nobody but you, Lord,*
b   *Nobody but you.*

Another similarity parallels *Blessed Be the Name of the Lord*. The Stanza development involves the insertion of a single phrase. In Job's story, two phrases are inserted but the basic structure is the same. In *Nobody But You, Lord*, the phrase *When I was a sinner...* is the first insertion but the frame of the piece remains unchanged. The two-line insertion in *Blessed* does not alter the Job narrative either. This device lends the hymn to added improvisation so long as the meter count of the syllables remains identical. Conversely, the Job hymn is restricted to the biblical story.

The form of this hymn is somewhat rare but the modal form of the melody gives it an attractiveness that will ensure its survival. Additionally, the presence of incremental iteration (repetition of the lyric line and melodic line) faciltates the ease for communal use. The inherent message will encourage enthusiastic participation.

Contemporary Significance

Here in the West, we are inundated with the technology of our time. Computers, satellites, supersonic planes, moon shots, laser surgery, etc., have induced in too many Christians the subconscious sentiment that God is old-fashioned. Some of the technology of our world is truly marvelous and mind-boggling, but there is no substitute for God!

Even in the arena of organized religion, the hucksters of the so-called *gospel of prosperity* have persuaded too many confessing Christians to succumb to crass materialism in the name of superficial piety. This hymn accentuates the great need for the *corpus Christo* — the body of Christ — to return to basics, full trust and dependence on God.

Irrespective of advanced technology and our alleged high standard of living, we need to be reminded that humans do not possess any measure of self-sufficiency. There is the additional consideration of the vicissitudes of human existence that affects all life on a non-discriminatory basis. Unlisted phone numbers and private post office boxes cannot deter trouble from finding out where we live. There is great reassurance in knowing that there is someone available to help us along this uneven pilgrimage of life.

Notes

1. Psalm 40:1-4
2. Wyatt Tee Walker, *The Dynamics of Afro-centric Christian Faith* The Stone Lectures: Averett Christian College, Danville, VA.
3. Wyatt Tee Walker, *Spirits That Dwell in Deep Woods I* (N.Y.: Martin Luther King Fellows Press, 1987), p.8.

SPIRITUAL WARFARE

SATAN, WE'RE GONNA' TEAR YOUR KINGDOM DOWN

Sa-tan , we're gon-na tear your king-dom down____

Sa-tan , we're gon-na tear your king-dom down____ you've been

build-ing up your king-dom ____ all ov-er this world ____

Sa-tan , we're gon-na tear your king-dom down____

Notations are charted as sung by Silver Strands

SATAN, WE'RE GONNA' TEAR YOUR KINGDOM DOWN

Refrain

Satan, we're gonna' tear your kingdom down.
Satan, we're gonna' tear your kingdom down;
You been building up your kingdom
All over this world,
Satan, we're gonna' tear your kingdom down.

Satan, we're gonna' sing your kingdom down.
Satan, we're gonna' sing your kingdom down;
You been building up your kingdom
All over this world,
Satan, we're gonna' sing your kingdom down.

Deacons gonna' pray your kingdom down.
Deacons gonna' pray your kingdom down;
You been building up your kingdom
All over this world,
Deacons gonna' pray your kingdom down.

Preachers gonna' preach your kingdom down.
Preachers gonna' preach your kingdom down;
You been building up your kingdom
All over this world,
Preachers gonna' preach your kingdom down.

Righteous gonna' shout your kingdom down.
Righteous gonna' shout your kingdom down;
You been building up your kingdom
All over this world,
Righteous gonna' shout your kingdom down.

5

SPIRITUAL WARFARE

Satan, We're Gonna' Tear Your Kingdom Down

Introduction

Not many people in our modern era subscribe to belief in a personal Devil. However, careful reading of the New Testament reveals clearly that Satan personalized his work through human beings. It is a recurring theme of the New Testament in Pauline literature as well as in the Gospels. Jesus himself, at several points, speaks of Satan in a personal sense. There is, of course, the classic narrative of Jesus' *Temptation in the Wilderness.*[1] In the last exchange, Jesus' response to the Satan's ploy to have our Lord worship him was, *Get thee behind me Satan...* Given the context of Christian belief and its reliance on the tradition of Scripture, it is not far-fetched to understand the spiritual genius of the originators of this particular *Prayer and Praise Hymn.* Though mention of Satan (or the Devil) is scarce in the Old Testament, the reader is reminded of the Creation narratives and the story of Job.[2]

Thus, it is altogether appropriate that in this genre of music to find such a hymn that personalizes the forces of evil in the world. The reality is that we *wrestle not against flesh and blood, but against principalities and powers...*[3] As authentic as the musical expression of any other theme of Christian faith, this hymn does no violence whatsoever as a bearer of another fundamental tenet of Christian faith.

Satan, indeed, has been *building up his kingdom all over this world!* The task of Christian disciples is to establish the kingdom of heaven on earth. Conversely, that means tearing down the kingdom of Satan in this world.

Biblical Basis

The Biblical tradition of personalizing evil in this world has already been mentioned at the beginning of this chapter. The *Temptation* narrative is perhaps the clearest example in New Testament literature of this phenomenon. The exchange between Simon Peter and the Lord on the occasion of the disciple's protest against our Lord's prophecy of the pending Cross is yet another example. John's Gospel quotes Jesus as declaring that Judas was *a devil.*[4] The most dramatic, of course, is in the Book of Revelation where Satan is ultimately cast in *the lake of fire,* symbolic of his utter defeat.[5]

There is much to choose from for this hymn's biblical roots because the tradition is so broad. However, for the purposes of this typology, the *Temptation* narrative seems best suited since our Lord's resistance to the wiles of the Devil shaped clearly the character of his ministry to humankind. The first temptation that the Satan proposed (stones into bread) would have made Jesus' movement a grand welfare state. Stones were in ample supply and there were more than enough hungry people who would be attracted in order to survive nutritionally. The second temptation centered in the exploitation of the divine powers inherent in the Incarnate Word — Jesus Christ. Here again, humankind would be seized by the display of supposed magical powers. The third and final temptation was intended to reduce the mission of the Master to earthly conquest, completely inimical to the spiritual kingdom that He came to establish.[6]

This hymn reveals the clear perception of its authors who grasped that which was at the center of the mission and message of Jesus, the establishment of the Father's kingdom in the hearts of men and women in this world in preparation for the next world.

Theological Mooring

One of the things that is apparent about the nature of God is that He hates sin. The author of sin in the world is *the Evil One*. That reference along with several others in the Bible is a characterization consistent with the Scriptures giving *persona* to the presence and work of evil in the world. The Adam and Eve narrative is perhaps the single instance where the will of God was violated by an animal figure, the serpent. The heart of the story maintains its theological integrity. The banishment of Adam and Eve from the garden of Eden had very little to do with eating the fruit, *per se*. It had to do with disobeying the will of God.[7] Disobedience is sin or literally from the Hebrew, *missing the mark*.

The struggle of humankind against sin whose legitimate parent is evil repeatedly takes on the *persona* mentioned above as *Satan, the Devil, the Evil One*, etc. The effect has been to give focus and dramatic attention to this pervasive presence of evil. For devotees of the Lord Jesus Christ, the consciousness is seared with instances of God's continuing displeasure and hostility to sin, the product of *the Evil One*.

It is the unsuccesful struggle of humankind against sin that precipitated our need for a Saviour. The Apostle Paul's treatise to the Roman church includes specifically that Jesus Christ (for those who trust in Him) frees us not only from Wrath, the Law and Death, but especially from Sin.[8] In Paul's view of our justification, our *righteousness is* achieved through faith in Jesus Christ, frees us from the power and dominance of sin because of that which God did in Christ at Calvary.[9] The Incarnate Christ by his coming into the world has put sin and Satan to rout. We who are His disciples are in turn empowered to overcome the power of sin in our personal and collective lives and consequently, overcome Satan himself. Thus, the theological mooring of this *Prayer and Praise Hymn* is indubitably sound in its central thrust. The task of the Christian is to *sing, pray, preach* and *shout* until Satan's kingdom in this world *comes tumbling down*.

Lyric and Form Analysis

Once again we have a slight variation in poetic form so common to this family of music. Upon reflection, it may very well be that these ever-so-slight variations are evidence of the spontaniety present in the formation of this music. Whatever the message expressed, the collective witness of the faith-community utilized whatever was at hand, musically and poetically, in order to get the message across.

> *a*   *Satan, we're gonna' tear your kingdom down.*
> *a*   *Satan, we're gonna' tear your kingdom down;*
> *b*   *You been building up your kingdom*
> *c*   *All over this world,*
> *a*   *Satan, we're gonna' tear your kingdom down.*

It would be possible to consider the *b* and *c* lines as a single line which would restore the form to the frequent appearing *a a b a* form. However, that seems to destroy the basic symmetry of the piece. Therefore, the slightly varied form seems to be the poetic form with which the originators were comfortable.

The music-piece in its melodic structure hold nothing especially distinctive. Its melodic line has the fundamental incremental iteration (melodic and lyric line repeating) so necessary for communal singing and preservation via the oral tradition. One refrain of the hymn sung in the presence of others is readily available for participation by everyone in the assembly. The stanza content moves from the general task to the specific tasks to suggest clearly that everyone must be engaged in the spiritual warfare against Satan.

Contemporary Significance

The quaintness of the *Prayer and Praise Hymn* at first glance might obscure what it is really about. The *Satan* reference arrests the attention immediately in much the same way the hyperbole in Oriental literature arrests attention. Though the focus is tearing Satan's kingdom down, the task undertaken has more to do with the nature of discipleship. Confessing Christians need to be reminded that our task is the persistent and unrelenting struggle against Satan and his works. Our modernity has seduced us into camouflaging sin with verbiage that is more *civilized!* Some years ago, Dr. Karl Menninger, the famous physician and psychiatrist, authored a book entitled, *Whatever Became of Sin!* He perceived our western propensity to camouflage sin. Our world sorely needs a sense of sin. It is akin to Flip Wilson's character, Geraldine who confessed frequently that *the Devil made me do it!* Ignoring and/or camouflaging sin will not make it disappear. An African-American colloquialism says succinctly, *the Devil is busy all the time!*

This hymn lifts up the sure and true challenge of discipleship. Our task as Christians is to wage a never-ending warfare against Satan and his works. *For we wrestle not against flesh and blood, but against principalities and powers, against the rulers of darkness of this world, against spiritual wickedness in high places.*[10]

Notes

1. Matthew 4:3ff.
2. Job 1:6
3. Ephesians 6:12
4. John 6:70,71
5. Revelation 20:10
6. Matthew 4:1ff.
7. Genesis 3:1ff.
8. Romans chapters 5-8
9. Romans 6:18
10. Ephesians 6:12

YOU BETTER MIN'

Notations are charted as sung by Silver Strands

YOU BETTER MIN'

Chorus:

You better min',
O you better min',
You got to give an account in the judgment,
You better min'.

Sister, you better min' how you talk,
You better min' what you talkin' about,
You got to give an account in the judgment,
You better min'.

Brother, you better min' how you pray,
You better min' what you prayin' about.
You got to give an account in the judgment,
You better min'.

Preacher, you better min' how you preach,
You better min' what you preachin' about,
You got to give an account in the judgment,
You better min'.

6

BE SAVED! BEHAVE!

You Better Min'

Introduction

This *Prayer and Praise Hymn* holds a lot of nostalgia for this writer. It conjures up clear memories of prayer meetings in the semi-rural flatlands of South Jersey. My father's small congregation was peopled by southerners from Virginia, North Carolina and Georgia. In the summertime, the windows of the frame church were open wide and the strains of old-time songs like this one filled the night air. The fervor and passion with which they were sung beckoned one's spirit as a magnet attracts metal. Fifty yards away you could pick out the voices of Aunt Sally Jones, Deacon Willie Beverly and Uncle Ed.[1] This *Prayer and Praise Hymn* was a warning that one had to live right to be a Christian. With their heads thrown back and their eyes closed, the message of this hymn jarred us into the reality of the demands of discipleship. Its message seemed ominous to our young and tender spirits. *O you better min'*...

Biblical Basis

The biblical tradition is clear; obedience is rewarded and disobedience is punished. In the Bible, this consideration is presented chiefly under the category of retribution. In return for obedience to his commands, God promises all

55

the good things humankind needs and craves. At the same time he gives warning that failure to do what he requires will bring disaster and death. This view is more characteristic of the Old Testament because it embraces the essence of the covenant-idea. However, there are some very explicit references in the New Testament that are just as pronounced. The biblical theme of retribution finds expression throughout the Scriptures. Thus any one of a number of explicit texts are suitable and applicable:

> *Be not decieved; God is not mocked:*
> *for whatsoever a man soweth, that*
> *shall he also reap. For he that*
> *soweth to the flesh shall of the flesh*
> *reap corruption; but that soweth to the*
> *Spirit shall of the Spirit reap life*
> *everlasting.*[2]

There is additionally, the parables of judgment (Matthew 25) each one with its own emphasis (the virgins, the talents and the sheep and the goats). There is one other Scripture, oft-quoted, which carries the same message of judgment: *For the wages of sin is death; but the gift of God is eternal life through Jesus Christ our Lord.*

It is fairly obvious that or foremothers and forefathers were not hardpressed to decipher this prevailing idea of judgment and retribution. Perhaps, more impressive is that they clearly perceived a connection between conduct and salvation which is at the heart of Paul's letter to the church at Rome. Salvation in Jesus Christ requires a companion code of behavior. It is a salvation ethic of righteous (godly) living.

Thelogical Mooring

The biblical concept of judgement (the word used explicitly and frequently in the music-piece under examination) is rooted in the covenant-idea. The covenant-idea developed out of the Biblical concept of Authority and Revelation. In the Bible itself, authority is more of what mgst be done than of what must be believed. Belief is secondary to action, though some belief is required because without belieh, man (woman) will not act. The New Testament puts much more stress than the Old Testament on what a person must believe to be saved, yet saving faith in the New Testament is not belief alone; it involves commitment and action. Biblical-based religion's first question is always, *What must I do?*[3]

That which must be done — the details — God reveals through the Bible. God's revelations are represented in the Bible in a series of covenants beginning with the covenant for the descendants of Noah with successive covenants with the patriarchs culminating with the covenant at Sinai. Judgment was pronounced on Israel because she failed to keep the covenant. It is from this Biblical concept that the idea of judgment developed.[4]

The Hebrew root meaning *to judge* and the words derived from it have a broader meaning than in corresponding English words: they include not only the pronouncement of sentence but also its execution.[5] It has to do with God's nature to establish justice.

This *Prayer and Praise Hymn* rather than being adjudged a *quaint religious ditty* must be recognized as a bearer of profound religious truth. It rises above the ordinary on two counts: it mirrors a great theological truth of the judgment to come over which God himself presides and more especially couches the warning of judgment that is based on conduct. It underscores the importance of behaviour for those of us who are candidates for the kingdom.

Lyric and Form Analysis

The poetic form of this hymn is the classic *a a b a* form that appears with great frequency in this genre of Black Sacred Music. How novel that the profound message that it carries moves on the vehicle most common to this family of musical expression. Perhaps the lesson is that the profound need not be complicated.

a	*You better min',*
a	*O you better min',*
b	*You got to give an account in the judgment,*
a	*You better min'.*

It is interesting to note that the stanza arrangement takes on a different poetic structure altogether. It is similar to the development of the stanza structure of *Till I Die.*[6] However, this hymn makes no attempt to use the couplet form whatsoever. Its stanzas are faithful to the theme of the hymn itself without being tempted to draw in anything that might be considered extraneous.

a	*Sister, you better min' how you talk,*
b	*You better min' what you talkin' about,*
c	*You got to give an account in the judgment,*
d	*You better min'.*

Some exception might be raised that the *a* and *b* lines of the stanzas are the same. They are very similar but not the same in the context of the music-piece itself. The *how* and the *what* of the stanza lines demand differentiation. The thematic line and the closing lines are distinct, thus the stanza form becomes *a b c* and *d*.

The melodic line is distinct and fits the general profile of this music. It has enough repetition for the easy replication necessary for communal use.

Contemporary Significance

There is some clear sense of the eschatological in this *Prayer and Praise Hymn.* That sense of pending judgment is needful in our times because of our tenacious hold on this life. We delude ourselves into believing that we are going to be here forever when the reality is that judgment is at hand in every breath we take. In spite of the clear admonition of our Lord that *no man knoweth the day or hour when the Son of man cometh,*[7] we persist in our loyalty to those things *which moth and rust doth corrupt.*[8]

It is a curious note that the warning of the first stanza focuses on loose talk — gossip — an activity we are too often prone to engage and consider harmless. Yet the hymn warns that we need to be careful of our talk and what we talk about. The second warning has to do with the desires of our hearts. We often pray for what we want and not what we need. It is instructive that that great caution must be exerted over the things we might be tempted to pray for. They might not be worthy of a prayer request. No wonder the saints of another era coined the folk-saying on prayer: *Lord teach us to pray and what to pray for.*

The third warning is to preachers. There is no constraint on truth. Sometimes preachers spend time on subjects that are not worthy of the listeners' time nor pleasing to God himself who calls preachers to preach. There is an ominous quality to this hymn. It stands in judgment of our everyday activity, it scrutinizes the innermost desires of our hearts and sits in judgment on the sayings of the preacherperson. We would do well to heed its bidding.

Notes

1. I Corinthians 15:17
2. I Corinthians 15:20
3. I Corinthians 15:49-52
4. Luke 20:27
5. Matthew 7:21
6. see *Introduction*, p. 2
7. Wyatt Tee Walker, *Somebody's Calling My Name* (Valley Forge: Judson Press, 1979), p. 57
8. Job 3:17

GLORY BOUND

I WANNA' DIE EASY

Min' _____ you bet-ter min' _____ you got to

You bet-ter min' You bet-ter min' you got to

give an ac-count in the judgement You bet-ter min' _____ sis-ter, you bet-ter

Give an ac-count in the judgement you better min' _____

Min' how you talk ____ you better min' what you're talking a-bout you got to

give an ac-count in the judgement you bet-ter min' _____ D.S.

Notations are charted as sung by Silver Strands

I WANNA' DIE EASY

I wanna die ea_____sy when I die_____ when I die_____ I wanna die

ea_____sy when I die_____ when I die I wan-na die

ea-sy when I die_____ Shout "Sal-va-tion" as I fly_____ I wan-na die

ea_____sy when I die_____ when I die I wan-na die

Notations are charted as sung by Silver Strands

I WANNA' DIE EASY

Refrain

> I wanna' die easy when I die (when I die).
> I wanna' die easy when I die (when I die).
> I wanna' die easy when I die;
> Shout "Salvation!" as I fly;
> I wanna' die easy when I die.

> I wanna' go to heaven when I die (when I die).
> I wanna' go to heaven when I die (when I die).
> I wanna' go to heaven when I die;
> Shout "Salvation!" as I fly;
> I wanna' die easy when I die.

> Gonna' shout "Troubles over!" when I die (when I die).
> Gonna' shout "Troubles over!" when I die (when I die).
> Gonna' shout "Troubles over!" when I die;
> Shout "Salvation!" as I fly;
> I wanna' die easy when I die.

> Wanna' see ma' Jesus when I die (when I die).
> Wanna' see ma' Jesus when I die (when I die).
> Wanna' see ma' Jesus when I die;
> Shout "Salvation!" as I fly;
> I wanna' die easy when I die.

> Wanna' see my mother when I die (when I die).
> Wanna' see my mother when I die (when I die).
> Wanna' see my mother when I die
> Shout "Salvation!" as I fly;
> I wanna' die easy when I die.

7

GLORY BOUND

I Wanna' Die Easy

Introduction

At first blush, it would appear this hymn is about death. Though it secondarily underscores the inevitability of that universal experience of all humanity, it is more about the assurance of immortality. The *die easy* reference infers the confidence of the faithful in the face of death. A part of the genius of this religious folk-music is the economy of language by which profound ideas are transmitted. As the hymn progresses, its confident declaration, *Shout salvation as I fly* reveals unshakeable faith in eternal life throught Jesus Christ. This specific conclusion can be deduced from the later verse, *Wanna' see ma' Jesus...* In less than ten lines, the linch-pin tenet of Christian faith is addressed within the framework of this brief hymn-poem.

The author was introduced to this *Prayer and Praise Hymn* in the late Sixties by the Chairman of the Board of the Canaan Baptist Church of Christ in Harlem, New York, Elmo Cooper. Deacon Cooper is a native of St. Petersburg, Florida and is a veritable *walking treasure* of this genre of Black Sacred Music. The presumption is that the geographical origin of this gem is the southeastern region of the United States.

Biblical Basis

The constant and accurate profile of this family of sacred music precludes that none are without either the implicit or explicit rootage in the Scriptures. This hymn, as all others, is anchored in the Holy Bible. For this writer, it is a clue to their moral authority and endurance. Close scrutiny of these hymns will reveal again and again, the soundness of their theological message. Essentially, that soundness is rooted in its Bible-based message.

The thematic phrases, *heaven, Troubles over! Wanna' see ma' Jesus, etc., all point directly to the appropriate eschatological* expectation of the Christian devotee. It follows then, logically, that its Biblical basis can be presumed to be the clearest statement of faith on immortality, is posed in the rhetorical question of the Apostle himself:

> *And if Christ be not risen, then is our preaching vain, and your faith vain also.*[1]

Then, six verses later, the conclusive declaration:

> *But now is Christ risen from the dead and become the first fruits of them that slept.*[2]

The classic passage begins at v. 49:

> *And as we have borne the image of the earthy, we shall also bear the image of the heavenly. Now this I say brethren, that flesh and blood cannot inherit the kingdom of God; neither doth corruption inherit incorruption. Behold, I show you a mystery; we shall not all sleep, but we shall all be changed. In a moment, in the twinkling of an eye, at the last trumpet: for the trumpet shall sound, and the dead shall be raised incorruptible, and we shall all be changed.*[3]

Theological Mooring

Humankind's quest for personal immortality finds expression in many climes and cultures, ancient and modern. It is then, no surprise, that the quest is an intergral part of the Christian faith. Judaism, from which Christianity sprang, fostered the idea from its earliest beginnings. By the time of the Christian era, belief in the resurrection was only marred by some nuances of belief that differed from sect to sect. However, immortality of the soul was uncontested in Jewry save for the Sadducees.[4] The advent of the field preacher from Galilee continued the Jewish tradition of espousing the *kingdom of heaven* concept. Jesus and his religious adversaries, the scribes and Pharisees, differed sharply on the eligibility for the kingdom of heaven. The Pharisaic profile was narrow; kingdom eligibility was based on being Jewish, male and healthy. The carpenter from Nazareth came preaching a gospel of universal eligibility that turned on *doing the will of my Father in heaven.*[5] Jesus had no quarrel with the Pharisees about the character of the kingdom, only the basis for eligibility. It was, as certified in the Synoptic Gospels, the center-piece of his public ministry. Again and again, his preaching and teaching echoed the tenets of *kingdom* teaching. At the heart of the *kingdom of heaven* or *kingdom of God* idea is the presumption of eternal life. The subsequent Death and Resurrection of the Galilean made personal immortality the centerpiece of the Christian faith as it remains today.

It is not difficult to understand, given the sociology of pain common to all of African ancestry, that the development of religious faith in slavery and post-slavery times, would seize upon this tenet of faith above all others. Thus the practice of Christianity among New World Africans is generally characterized as *otherworldly*. Notwithstanding the accuracy of this judgment, it must be noted that all *world religions* are also *otherworldly* in character. It is then, some mark of spiritual genius, given the humble profile of the originators of this music, that their tenacious grasp of the idea of immortality finds expression in this hymn-poem.[6] The theological center and framework of this *Prayer and Praise Hymn* is without question, eternal life through Jesus Christ.

Lyric and Form Analysis

The *Introduction* to this volume provides some brief discussion about the narrow breadth of lyric form common to this music. The most frequent poetic forms are the *a a a b* and the *a a b a*. Most of the other forms that appear in this family of music are variations on the two mentioned here. This *Prayer and Praise Hymn* is a prime example of variation distinguished by the appearance of an additional or extra line.

a	*I wanna' die easy when I die (when I die).*
a	*I wanna' die easy when I die (when I die).*
a	*I wanna' die easy when I die;*
b	*Shout 'Salvation!' as I fly;*
a	*I wanna' die easy when I die.*

The musicality of this hymn belies the imprint of the *Spiritual* form. There is of course, the repetition common to all original music composed by Americans of African descent in the antebellum and postwar eras. The repetition is reinforced by another common trait of the *Spiritual*, that of incremental iteration, the repetition in the melodic line as well as in the lyric line.[7] That trait, as must be noted, is not rigid. The absence of absolute rigidity is what provides the musical color for this hymn.

There are three elements that contribute to the basic character of this particular hymn. The first is the manner with which the retarded emphasis is placed on the word *easy*. In the second and third lines, it is sung on a distinctly different note. The second element is the *Call and response* insertion in the first two lines that are carried throughout the hymn. The third element is the completely different modal form of the third line that leads into the *b* line. It is of some note that the first and last line adhere rigidly to the incremental iteration mentioned earlier.

The verbiage of the stanzas are consonant with the inherent theme. The progression from *heaven* to *Troubles over!* are clearly indicative of the eschatological content. The *Jesus* stanza merely confirms again the Christocentricity of the religious faith of African-Americans of the free Church. The *mother* reference in this type of hymn about the future life is a predictable sentiment that finds expression with great frequency. This is an important hymn of this genre of Black Sacred Music.

Contemporary Significance

There is a piece of folk-wisdom that borders on humor but is very revealing about the modern temper and the prospect of death. *Everybody wants to go to heaven but nobody wants to die!* In the West, particularly, there is increasing evidence that the public mind has a general disposition toward dodging death. The persistent glorification of youth and the extraordinary efforts to extend life in the medical arena are both symptoms of the unconscious, tenacious desire to hold on to physical life. The bizarre interest in freezing corpses by some high-profile Americans is yet another aberration of this notion. These symptoms, however deep, cannot deter in any wise the inevitable reality of death. The significance of this hymn is that, it will aid in dispelling the notion of humankind's invincibility against death.

This hymn not only serves to remind its hearers that death is a reality and unescapable but also engenders the hope and reality of eternal life through Jesus Christ. The *easy* reference is not only useful as a musical device as described earlier but also suggests what the comfort level of the Christian can be if trust of one's soul is deposited with Jesus Christ as Lord and Saviour. Whoever dies in Christ does so not as a ship ripped from its mooring by the storms and travails of this life, but rather as a ship whose sails are hoisted to catch the winds will transport us to that other land where Job declared, *the wicked shall cease from troubling and the weary shall be at rest.*[8]

Notes

1. Disciples of the Calvary Baptist Church, Merchantville, New Jersey
2. Galatians 6:7,8
3. Millar Burrows, *An Outline of Biblical Theology* (Philadelphia: Westminster Press, 1946), p. 10
4. *Ibid*, p. 11
5. *Ibid*, p. 173
6. see Chapter Three
7. Matthew 25:13
8. Matthew 6:19

CITY OF REFUGE

YOU BETTER RUN

Notations are charted as sung by Silver Strands

YOU BETTER RUN

thu-se-law, he was the old-est man___ He lived_____ nine hun-dred and

six-ty nine____And he died____and went to heaven in all due time____he had to

(SOLO) (CHOIR

run, had to run, had to run____ he had to run had to run had to

run he had to run to the ci-ty of re-fuge he had to

1. (SOLO 2.

run _____ You know run._____ you bet-ter run____

D.S. AL FINE

Aztec® PT - 8 R

DIAZ-TEC 500

YOU BETTER RUN

Refrain

You better run
better run
better run
You better run
better run
better run
You better run to the city of refuge
You better run

Stanza 1

If you don't believe that I'm singin' right
Just pick up your Bible and read it tonight
Just read in Genesis, you understand
That Methuselah he was the oldest man
He lived nine hundred and sixty-nine
And he died and went to heaven in all due time.

Altered refrain:

You know he had to run
had to run
had to run
Oh he had to run
had to run
had to run
Oh he had to run to the city of refuge
He had to run

Stanza 2

You know God called Moses on the mountaintop
He stamped his law right on Moses' heart
He put his commandments in Moses' mind
He said "Moses, don't you leave my children behind
I want you to lead them to the Promised Land
All you have to do is follow my command"

Stanza 3

God sent Jonah to Nineveh land
He didn't obey my Lord's command
Wind blew the ship from shore to shore
The whale swallowed Jonah and he was no more

Stanza 4

Read 'bout Samson from his birth
He was the strongest man on earth
Live 'way back in ancient times
And killed 'bout a thousand Philistines

8

CITE...
CITY OF REFUGE

You Better Run

Introduction

    This hymn is the rarest of the rare. No hymn in this family of Black Sacred Music compares in any way, poetic structure, form, musically, etc. It is obviously one of a kind. I tracked this hymn to the low country of South Carolina (south of Charleston) though I have no hard evidence that its roots are there. Countless inquiries, however, point to South Carolina origin. It is a *type* of Prayer and Praise Hymn. Its form was popularized by "singing preachers" who traveled the Southland prior to and immediately following World War I. They appeared in communities unannounced and made themselves available to sing at any religious gathering for the most modest of free-will offerings. They were distinguished because they did not preach so much as they *performed* as troubadours. Some have been knows to sing a song-type for a half an hour, all by rote, returning occasionally to a refrain that their audience could join. *You Better Run!* is of that genre.

    The only such "singing preacher" I can recall is Dr. J. H. Skipwith who was widely known all over the South and much of America. In the Fifties in Richmond, Virginia, I attended a revival service where he was the scheduled preacher. Skipwith's *sermon* was interspersed with at least eight to ten songs which came unannounced with very little reference to what he was allegedly preaching about. Without a doubt, Skipwith was a throwback to the "singing preachers" of an earlier era. Blessed with a clear tenor voice and a remarkable memory, Skipwith almost always sang *a capella*. He enjoyed a wide reputation for his musical skills and seemed welcome to any gathering, large or small. For many years he was the official song leader at the famed Hampton Ministers' Conference and his name is listed as a member of the Music Committee for the Baptist Standard Hymnal published by the National Baptist Convention, Inc.

Other than Skipwith, the only other "singing preacher" I encountered was in Frogmore. South Carolina during an SCLC retreat at the Penn Center. The gentleman was from St. Johns Island and in one evening session, he led a song with a chorus similar to *You Better Run!* My recollection is that his rendition, laced with Biblical references, seemed to have forty stanzas similar to the construct of this hymn. The rarity of this hymn is pronounced because it is the only one of its kind that, so far as I know, remains extant.

Biblical Basis

The *city of refuge* reference is easy to posit. In Numbers 35:23ff, the conditions of the city of refuge are made explicit.[1] In order to provide for the security of those, who unawares and without design should kill a man, the Lord commanded Moses to appoint six cities of refuge, that the manslayer might flee to and have time to prepare for justification before the judges, so that the kinsman of the deceased might not pursue him there and kill him. Of these cities, there were three on each side of the Jordan; those west of the Jordan were Kedesh of Naphtali, Hebron and Shechem. Those beyond Jordan (east) were Bezer, Golan and Ramoth Gilead.

These cities were to be easy of access and to have smooth and good roads to them, and bridges where necessary. When there were any crossroads, they took care to set up posts with an inscription, directing the way to the city of refuge. This city was to be well supplied with water and all kinds of provisions. The case then came before the judges, and if possible, he might clear himself. If he was found innocent, he dwelt safely in the city to which he had fled; if otherwise, he was put to death according to the severity of the law. Though he was found innocent, he was not immediately set at liberty, but he was obliged to dwell in this city without going out of it until the death of the high priest. And if before this time he should go anywhere out of the city, the avenger of blood might safely kill him.

It is patently clear that though the context of the hymn is the Biblical city of refuge, that is not the intent of the hymn's message. The theology of our ancestors created an overlay of the concept and it is presumed that the city of refuge is servanthood to God or discipleship in Jesus Christ, both of which are the same. In that sense, one has no city of refuge available if he or she has not made a commitment of faith. In lieu of pending judgment, the only one to turn to is the Lord himself, our personal *city of refuge.*

Theological Mooring

The theological mooring of this *Prayer and Praise Hymn* is anchored in a metaphor created by its originators. The section preceding makes clear the Biblical root of the idea. In their creativity, they never intended to suggest that there is actually a city of refuge, a *locus*, to which the hearers of this hymn might repair. Ever mindful of the pending and/or imminent judgment for the individual, the influence of Revelation is probable. The dramatic and descriptive images of the last days, e.g. Revelation 6ff. After the appearance of the Four Horsemen and the opening of the sixth seal, the judgment of the Lamb (the wrath to come) is so dreadful that:

> *the kings of the earth and the great men*
> *and the rich men and the chief captains*
> *and the mighty men and every bondman*
> *and every freeman, hid themselves in*
> *dens and in the rocks of the mountain.*
> *And said to the mountains and rocks,*
> *Fall on us and hide us from the face of*
> *him that sitteth on the throne and from*
> *the wrath of the Lamb.*[2]

With no hiding place, the admonition is to run to the city of refuge! Now the point of Revelation is that under the most intense persecution (reign of Domitian), the followers of Jesus Christ must remain faithful unto death in order to escape the wrath to come. My deduction is that the warning is intended to persuade the hearer to make a commitment to Jesus Christ. He is the city of refuge!

There's another old hymn that comes to mind:

> *There's no hiding place down here;*
> *There's no hiding place down here.*
> *I went to the rock*
> *To hide my face*
> *The rock cried out, 'No hiding place!*
> *There's no hiding place down!'*[3]

The perpetual crisis of their circumstance made them more sensitive to a sense of *eschatos*. They lived in the presence of imminent judgment always. It is probable that this sense of judgment and *eschatos* influenced the development of this hymn.

Lyric and Form Analysis

The melodic line of this *Prayer and Praise Hymn* is not particularly distinguished though it is a little odd. The double refrain and repetition set it apart. It is the stanza that draws attention. The stanzas are chanted rather than sung. It is the sing-song chant of the stanzas that gives character to the music-piece and adds the dimension of quaintness. In places the rhyme and meter is a little awkward and stilted. Even the rhyme at points is not smooth and the variation between six-line and four line stanzas invoke some curiosity. The beginning stanza is six lines as well as the Moses' stanza while the others are four lines only. I have no explanation for this except that it is a quirk of the oral tradition of this music. For the most part, the stanzas are a conglomeration of two line couplets that focus on disparate Bible themes and narratives, e.g. Methuselah, Moses, Jonah and Samson. There are probably many more stanzas that are no longer extant and much of what appears here is fragmentary which contributes to some of the unevenness.

The chorus, such as it is nearly matches the general profile though in performance, it is changed slightly to accomodate the shift from stanza to chorus (see lyrics).

a	*You better run*
	better run
	better run
a	*You better run*
	better run
	better run
b	*You better run to the city of refuge*
a	*You better run*

I have arbitrarily treated the repetition as a single line since there is no fundamental change in the lyric. This enables the poetic form to fit the classic *a a b a* form.

The stanza analysis is a little more difficult since it employs the rhyming couplets as over against repeating lines. For our purposes, let us use the rhyme as a guide to form, then it would appear as below.

a	*If you don't believe I'm singing right*
a	*Just pick up your Bible and read it tonight*
b	*Just read in Genesis, you understand*
b	*That Methuselah was the oldest man*
c	*You know he lived nine hundred and sixty-nine*
c	*And he died and went to heaven in all due time.*

The transition from stanza to chorus is as follows:

You know he had to run
had to run
had to run
Oh he had to run to the city of refuge
He had to run

This is the variation mentioned earlier to accommodate the maintenance of the rhythm and meter of the hymn.

Contemporary Significance

The message of this hymn is straightforward. We all live on the precipice of imminent judgment. That judgment is also ultimate. The prophecy of Revelation casts a long shadow that falls on the path of every human being. Thereby, each must have his or her city of refuge. The religious folk-wisdom is that *everyone must make his peace with God.* For devotees of the Christian faith, Jesus is our city of refuge and he provides shelter from all storms of life. It is to him that we can repair irrespective of what our lot in life may be. For any who never made a commitment to Jesus Christ in the pardon of their sins and accepted Him as personal Saviour, *You better run, better run, better run, You better run to the city of refuge, You better run!*

Notes

1. Alexander Cruden, *Cruden's Complete Concordance* (Philadelphia: John C. Winston, 1930), p. 534
2. Revelation 6:15,16
3. Traditional praise hymn